Pseud "Cavendish"

The Laws of Écarté

Adopted by the Turf and Portland Clubs

Pseud "Cavendish"

The Laws of Écarté
Adopted by the Turf and Portland Clubs

ISBN/EAN: 9783337233334

Printed in Europe, USA, Canada, Australia, Japan

Cover: Foto ©Andreas Hilbeck / pixelio.de

More available books at **www.hansebooks.com**

THE LAWS

OF

ÉCARTÉ

ADOPTED BY

THE TURF AND PORTLAND CLUBS

WITH

A TREATISE ON THE GAME

BY

"CAVENDISH"

AUTHOR OF

"THE LAWS AND PRINCIPLES OF WHIST"

ETC., ETC.

THIRD EDITION.

LONDON:

THOS. DE LA RUE & CO.

1886.

THE LAWS have been adopted by the undermentioned Clubs:—

TURF.	PORTLAND.
	AND
ARMY AND NAVY.	NEW UNIVERSITY.
ARTHUR'S.	OXFORD AND CAMBRIDGE
BOODLE'S.	RALEIGH.
BRIGHTON UNION.	REFORM.
CARLTON.	ST. JAMES'.
CONSERVATIVE.	ST. JAMES' WHIST.
DEVONSHIRE.	TRAVELLERS'.
E. I. UNITED SERVICE.	UNION.
GARRICK.	UNITED UNIVERSITY.
GUARDS'.	UNITED WHIST.
HANOVER SQUARE.	WESTMINSTER.
JUNIOR ATHENÆUM.	WHITEHALL.
JUNIOR CARLTON.	WHITE'S.
NAVAL AND MILITARY.	WINDHAM.

1st May, 1878.

THE LAWS OF ÉCARTÉ.

The want of a recognised Code of Écarté Laws as been long felt. The favourable reception accorded the Laws of Whist, edited by Mr. Baldwin, and those of Piquet, edited by "Cavendish," induced ie former gentleman to propose to the Turf Club adopt some revised Laws of Écarté, edited by Cavendish." The proposition was acceded to *m. con.*

The revision was superintended by the following carté Laws Committee :—

JOHN LORAINE BALDWIN, Esq.
(Chairman.)

| HE EARL OF ORFORD. | RUSSELL D. WALKER, Esq. |
| ENRY JONES, Esq. | ROBERT WHEBLE, Esq. |

At the General Meeting of the Turf Club held ay 28th, 1877, the Code prepared by the above ommittee, and edited by "Cavendish," was adopted.

The Portland Club, on being requested also t‹ dopt these Laws, snggested to the Écarté Laws Com ittee a slight alteration, which was immediately an‹ nanimously accepted; and the Portland Clnb gav ieir adhesion to the Code on July 6th, 1877.

PORTLAND CLUB,
July. 1877.

SHUFFLING.

1. Each player has a right to shuffle both his own and his adversary's pack. The dealer has the right to shuffle last.

2. The pack must not be shuffled below the table, nor in such a manner as to expose the faces of the cards, nor during the play of the hand.

CUTTING.

3. A cut must consist of at least two cards, and at least two must be left in the lower packet.

4. A player exposing more than one card, when cutting for deal, must cut again.

5. The player who cuts the highest Écarté card deals, and has choice of cards and seats. The choice determines both seats and cards during the play.

6. The cut for deal holds good even if the pack be incorrect.

7. If in cutting to the dealer a card be exposed,

DEALING.

8. The dealer must give five cards to his adversary and five to himself, by two at a time to each, and then by three at a time to each, or *vice versâ*. The dealer having selected the order in which he will distribute the cards must not change it during that game; nor may he change it at the commencement of any subsequent game, unless he inform the non-dealer before the pack is cut.

9. If the dealer give more or less than five cards to his adversary, or to himself, or do not adhere to the order of distribution first selected, and the error be discovered before the trump card is turned, the non-dealer, before he looks at his hand, may require the dealer to rectify the error, or may claim a fresh deal.

10. The hands having been dealt, the dealer must turn up for trumps the top card of those remaining.

11. If the dealer turn up more than one card, the non-dealer, before he looks at his hand, may choose which of the exposed cards shall be the trump, or may claim a fresh deal. Should the non-dealer have looked at his hand there must be a fresh deal.

12. If, before the trump card is turned up, a faced card be discovered in the pack, there must be a fresh deal.

13. If the dealer expose any of his own cards, the deal stands good. If he expose any of his adversary's cards, the non-dealer, before he looks at his hand, may claim a fresh deal.

14. If a player deal out of his turn, or with his adversary's pack, and the error be discovered before the trump card is turned up, the deal is void. After the trump card is turned up it is too late to rectify the error, and, if the adversary's pack has been dealt with, the packs remain changed.

15. If, after the trump card is turned up, and before proposing, or, if there is no proposal, before playing, it be discovered that the non-dealer has more than five cards, he may claim a fresh deal. Should the non-dealer not claim a fresh deal, he discards the superfluous cards, and the dealer is not entitled to see them.

16. If, after the trump card is turned up, and before proposing, or, if there is no proposal, before playing, it be discovered that the non-dealer has less than five cards, he may have his hand completed from the stock, or may claim a fresh deal.

17. If, after the trump card is turned up, and before the dealer accepts or refuses, or, if there is no proposal, before he plays, it be discovered that he has dealt himself more than five cards, the non-dealer may claim a fresh deal. Should he not claim a fresh deal, he draws the superfluous cards from the dealer's hand. Should the dealer have taken up his hand, the non-dealer is entitled to look at the cards he draws.

18. If, after the trump card is turned up, and before the dealer accepts or refuses, or, if there is no proposal, before he plays, it be discovered that the dealer has less than five cards, the non-dealer may permit the dealer to complete his hand from the stock or may claim a fresh deal.

19. If a fresh deal be not claimed when the wrong number of cards are dealt, the dealer cannot mark the king turned up.

20. If the non-dealer play without taking cards and it be then discovered that he has more or less than five cards, there must be a fresh deal.

21. If the dealer play without taking cards, and it be then discovered that he has more or less than five cards, his adversary may claim a fresh deal.

MARKING THE KING.

22. If a king be turned up, the dealer is entitled to mark it at any time before the trump card of the next deal is turned up.

23. If either player hold the king of trumps, he must announce it before playing his first card, or he loses the right to mark it. It is not sufficient to mark the king held in hand without announcing it.

24. If the king be the card first led, it may be announced at any time prior to its being played to. If the king be the card first played by the dealer he may announce it at any time before he play again.

25. If a player not holding the king announce it and fail to declare his error before he has played a card, the adversary may correct the score and has the option of requiring the hands to be played over again notwithstanding that he may have abandoned his hand. If the offender win the point, he marks nothing; if he win the vole, he marks only one; if he win the point when his adversary has played without proposing, or

has refused the first proposal he marks only one. But if the adversary himself hold the king, there is no penalty.

PROPOSING, ACCEPTING, AND REFUSING.

26. If a player propose he cannot retract; nor can he alter the number of cards asked for.

27. The dealer having accepted or refused cannot retract. The dealer, if required, must inform his adversary how many cards he has taken.

DISCARDING.

28. Each player, before taking cards, must put his discard face downward on the table, apart from the stock, and from his adversary's discard. Cards once discarded must not be looked at.

29. If the non-dealer take more cards than he has discarded, and mix any of them with his hand, the dealer may claim a fresh deal. If the dealer elect to play the hand, he draws the superfluous cards from the non-dealer's hand. Should the non-dealer have taken up any of the cards given him, the dealer is entitled to look at the cards he draws.

30. If the non-dealer ask for less cards than he has discarded, the dealer counts as tricks all cards which cannot be played to.

31. If the dealer give his adversary more cards than he has asked for, the non-dealer may claim a fresh deal. If the non-dealer elect to play the hand, he discards the superfluous cards, and the dealer is not entitled to see them.

32. If the dealer give his adversary less cards than he has asked for, the non-dealer may claim a fresh deal. If the non-dealer elect to play the hand, he has it completed from the stock.

33. If the dealer give himself more cards than he has discarded, and mix any of them with his hand, the non-dealer may claim a fresh deal. If the non-dealer elect to play the hand, he draws the superfluous cards from the dealer's hand. Should the dealer have taken up any of the cards he has given himself, the non-dealer is entitled to look at the cards he draws.

34. If the dealer give himself less cards than he has discarded, he may, before playing, complete his hand from the stock. If the dealer play with less than five cards, the non-dealer counts as tricks all cards which cannot be played to.

35. If a faced card be found in the stock after discarding, both players have a right to see it. The faced card must be thrown aside, and the next card given instead.

36. If, in giving cards, any of the non-dealer's are exposed, he has the option of taking them. Should the non-dealer refuse them, they must be thrown aside, and the next cards given instead. If the dealer expose any of his own cards, he must take them.

37. If, after giving cards, the dealer turn up a card in error, as though it were the trump card, he cannot refuse another discard. If another be demanded, the non-dealer has the option of taking the exposed card.

38. If the dealer accept when there are not sufficient cards left in the stock to enable the players to

exchange as many cards as they wish, the non-dealer is entitled to exchange as many as he asked for, or, if there are not enough, as many as there are left, and the dealer must play his hand. The dealer is at liberty to accept conditionally on there being cards enough in the stock.

PLAYING.

39. A card led in turn cannot be taken up again. A card played to a lead may be taken up again to save a revoke or to correct the error of not winning a trick when able, and then only prior to another card being led.

40. If a card be led out of turn, it may be taken up again, prior to its being played to. After it has been played to the error cannot be rectified.

41. If the leader name one suit and play another, the adversary may play to the card led, or may require the leader to play the suit named. If the leader have none of the suit named, the card led cannot be withdrawn.

42. If a player abandon his hand when he has not made a trick, his adversary is entitled to mark the vole. If a player abandon his hand after he has made one or two tricks, his adversary is entitled to mark the point. But, if a player throw down his cards, claiming to score, the hand is not abandoned, and there is no penalty.

REVOKING AND NOT WINNING THE TRICK.

43. If a player renounce when he holds a card of the suit led, or if a player fail to win the trick when

able, his adversary has the option of requiring the hands to be played again, notwithstanding that he may have abandoned his hand.   If the offender win the point he marks nothing; if he win the vole he marks only one; if he win the point when his adversary has played without proposing or has refused the first proposal, he marks only one.   Should the card played in error be taken up again prior to another card being led, (as provided by Law 39), there is no penalty.

CALLING FOR NEW CARDS.

44. A player may call for new cards at his own expense, at any time before the pack is cut for the next deal. He must call for two new packs, of which the dealer has choice.

INCORRECT PACKS.

45. If a pack be discovered to be incorrect, redundant, or imperfect, the deal in which the discovery is made is void.   All preceding deals stand good.

SCORING.

46. The game is five up.   By agreement the game may count a treble if the adversary has not scored; a double, if he has scored one or two; a single, if he has scored three or four.

47. A player turning up a king, or holding the king of trumps in his hand, is entitled to mark one.

48. A player winning the point is entitled to mark one; a player winning the vole is entitled to mark two.

49. If the non-dealer play without proposing, and fail to win the point, his adversary is entitled to mark two.   If the dealer refuse the first proposal, and fail to win the point, the non-dealer is entitled to mark two. These scores apply only to the first proposal or refusal in a hand, and only to the point, the score for the vole being unaffected.

50. If a player omit to mark his score, he may rectify the omission at any time before the trump card of the next deal is turned up.

51. An admitted overscore can be taken down at any time during the game.

BYSTANDERS.

52. If the players declare to play English Écarté, bystanders, whether betting or not, are not allowed to make any remark; nor to draw attention to errors in the score; nor to advise on the play; nor to play out the game of a player who resigns.

53. Bystanders at English Écarté calling attention to any error or oversight, and thereby affecting the score, may be called upon to pay all stakes and bets of the player whose interest is prejudicially affected. A bystander, by agreement between the players, may decide any question.

54. At French Écarté those covering the stakes may draw attention to errors in the score; may advise the player they are backing; or may play out the game of a player who resigns. Advice must be given by pointing only; neither cards nor suit may be named. The player is at liberty to follow the advice or not.

55. Bettors must not look over the hand of a player against whom they are betting.

A TREATISE ON ÉCARTÉ

BY

"CAVENDISH."

B

TO

JOHN LORAINE BALDWIN,

(Chairman of the Écarté Laws Committee, 1877),

THIS

Treatise on Écarté

IS

CORDIALLY DEDICATED

BY

HIS SINCERE FRIEND,

THE AUTHOR.

ÉCARTÉ.

THE GAME OF ÉCARTÉ in some of its features, namely, the discard (from which its name is derived), and the score for the king, is of modern origin; but, in other respects, it is so like the ancient game of *La Triomphe* that there can scarcely be a doubt the one is a development of the other. Paul Boiteau d'Ambly ("*Les Cartes à Jouer*," Hachette, Paris, 1854,) takes the same view. He says: "*La triomphe. Ce jeu est le père de l'écarté;*" and again "*l'écarté, modification de la triomphe.*"

La Triomphe (so called on account of the predominance of the trump suit, or suit of triumph,) is supposed to be one of the oldest of card games, possibly coming next after the games played with *tarots*, which are the earliest of all. *Trionfi* is mentioned by Berni ("*Capitolo del Gioco della Primera,*") in 1526. Berni states that the game was played by the peasants. In some Latin and French dialogues written by a Spaniard named Vives (d. 1541) there is an interesting one respecting a card party playing at *Triumphus Hispanicus.* If these were the same as the game of *La Triomphe*, as seems probable, the generally received statement that it is of French origin should be received with some caution. About the same time (1545) Rabelais finished his "Gargantua and Pantagruel," though some of it was published earlier. In the list of games there given *La Triomphe* is included ; so, whether a French game or not, it may be inferred that it had already an accepted French name.

The earliest French description of the game occurs in "*La Maison Académiqve*" (Paris, 1659). "*La Maison*" was reprinted under the title of "*La Maison des Ievx Académiqves*," and was finally transformed into the "*Académie Universelle des Jeux*," and *La Triomphe* appears, but slightly altered, in the many editions published between the middle of the seventeenth and the beginning of the nineteenth century, when it dropped out and was succeeded by Écarté.

La Triomphe was played in several ways, either *tête-à-tête*, or with partners, or as a round game. The packs consisted of the same cards as now, all the small cards from the six to the deuce being removed. The ace ranked between the knave and ten, except in one variety of the game.

When played with partners two against two, or less frequently (*quelquefois même*) three against three, those who cut together sat on one side of the table, and their adversaries on the other side, and the partners were allowed to communicate their game to each other by showing their hands only, advice by word of mouth not being permitted.

Whether playing singly or with partners the players had to cut for deal, the lowest dealing, and they played in the order in which they sat; each side, at the partner game, it is to be presumed, playing alternately one card at a time.

Five cards were dealt by two and by three at a time to each player. Originally the number dealt was a matter of agreement (*convenu*). The top card of the stock was turned up for trumps, and placed face upwards on the stock.

The eldest hand then led any card he thought proper; the other players were obliged to follow suit, to win the trick if able, and, having none of the suit led, to trump if able. If a trick was trumped, the after players, holding trumps and not being able to follow suit, were compelled to play trumps, even though their highest trump was lower than the one previously played.

The player or side that made three tricks marked one point (*marque un jeu*, erroneously translated "game" by some writers); and similarly, the vole was marked two. The game was usually five up, but originally the number of points to be made to win the game was decided by agreement.

If one side (or player at the *tête-à-tête* game,) were not satisfied with their hands, they were at liberty to offer the point to the adversary. If the offer was refused, the adversary was bound to win the vole, on penalty, if he failed, of having two scored against him.

In the *Encyclopédie Méthodique*, *Dictionnaire des Jeux Mathématiques* (Paris, 1798-9), a problem is given, showing the proper play with a certain hand when

the point was offered.   It runs thus :—" PROBLÉME.
Pierre et Paul jouent en cinq points à la triomphe; *ils
en ont chacun* trois : *Pierre est le premier ; il a le roi
et la dame troisième de triomphe, qui sera, par exemple
de trèfle, et un roi de carreau gardé par le valet :
lorsqu'on joue son roi de triomphe pour la première
carte, Paul lui offre un point.   On demande s'il le doit
accepter, et quelle est, en le refusant, son espérance de
faire la volle.*"   The answer given is that it is to
Pierre's advantage (as is clear) to refuse; and the
calculation of his chance of winning the vole is added.

When *La Triomphe* was played as a round game
(*que chaque Joueur joue pour soi*), four or five usually
constituted the table.   If two players each made two
tricks, the one that made the first two scored the
point.   The *Académie* does not say what happened if
no one made two tricks.

There was another variety of the game in which the
ace was sometimes the highest card, but sometimes
retained its rank between knave and ten.   If the
dealer turned up an ace he could *pillage, i.e.,* take the
turn-up card into his hand, and discard one card.
He could also look at the card immediately following
on the top of the stock ; if a trump, he could again
pillage that, and so on, until he came to a card of a
different suit.   Similarly, if one of the players had the
ace of trumps in his hand, he could pillage.   This
mode of playing was called *jouer à l'as qui pille.*   In
some editions of the *Académie* it is stated that the
round game might be played "*à l'as qui ne pille
point.*"   .

The close resemblance between *La Triomphe* and Écarté clearly appears from this description. There was a somewhat similar game, but not so old as *La Triomphe*, called *l'Homme d'Auvergne*, where the king was marked as at Écarté. In this game there was also a kind of substitute for discarding, in that, if none of the players liked their hands, there might be a second turn-up, and, if this suited no one, there might be a third turn-up, but not a fourth.

The game of *La Triomphe* is shortly described in Cotton's " Compleat Gamester " (London, 1674), under the name of French-Ruff, to distinguish it from Ruff-and-Honours. The latter was a game very like the English game of Trump, the forerunner of Whist; indeed one may say that *La Triomphe*, French-Ruff, and Écarté stand in the same relation to each other as Trump (English), Ruff-and-Honours, and Whist. Cotton's account of French-Ruff is repeated in every edition up to 1709, after which the book was incorporated with Seymour's "Court Gamester," the two being published together under Cotton's title, and French-Ruff appears there in all editions, and almost *verbatim* with the original text of Cotton, as late as the third quarter of the eighteenth century. Cotton says :—" CHAP. XI. *French-Ruff*.—You may play either two, four, or six of a side [this appears to be a mistake, as, according to the *Académie*, the game was seldom played more than two of a side, and often *tête-à-tête;* in Seymour's editions 'four or six of a side'], dealing to each five a piece, either two first at a time, or three, according to pleasure, and he that

deals turns up Trump; the King is the highest Card
at Trumps, and so it is highest in all other Cards that
are not Trumps, the Queen is next, the Knave next,
and next to that the Ace, and all other Cards follow
in preheminency according to the number of the Pips,
but all small Trumps win the highest of any other
suit."

After explaining pillaging "if so agreed amongst
the Gamesters," Cotton continues :—"After this they
play : to win two tricks signifies nothing, to win three
or four wins but one, but to win five is the winning of
five [probably a misprint for two, but repeated so in
all the editions of both Cotton and Seymour]. * * *
You are bound to follow suit, and if you renounce or
renege, you lose the whole Game, if you so make it,
otherwise but one or two according to agreement.
He that plays a Card that is trumped by the follower,
if the next player hath none of the former suit he
must trump it again, although he hath never a trump
in his hand that can win the former trump, and so it
must pass to the last player. All the Players round
are bound to win the highest trump play'd if they
can."

There is negative evidence that the game of *La
Triomphe* remained without material alteration up to
the beginning of the nineteenth century, for it con-
stantly appears in books on games and in works
of reference, while Écarté does not. Thus, in the
Dictionnaire de l'Académie Française (fifth edition,
published in 1798-9,) there is no mention of Écarté;
but in the sixth edition (published in 1835) it finds a

place. Again, in the *Encyclopédie Méthodique* (1798-9), which contains Whist, a game unknown in France until after Hoyle's time (second half of eighteenth century), there is *La Triomphe*, but no Écarté. The same remarks apply to the *Académie des Jeux* of 1805. Hoyle never wrote about Écarté, nor is the game included in any of the numerous Improved (?) Hoyles which were published after his death up to 1817. It is added in the edition of 1826 (revised and corrected by Charles Jones, Esq., London), and in all subsequent editions.

The exact time at which Écarté took the place of *La Triomphe* must remain a matter of conjecture. As Paul Boiteau (*Cartes à Jouer*) well remarks, "It is impossible to say of any game that it was invented in any particular year. Sometimes one person, sometimes another, proposes the addition of certain rules to an old game, and to change its name. Friends adopt it; it spreads; and thus a new game is invented." Boiteau does not assign any date to the introduction of Écarté, but places it in his third division of games, which were first played after the time of Louis XIV, *i.e.*, not earlier than 1715. He says, "it is a game entirely French, and to my mind one of the most pleasant of games, extremely difficult to play well and to win at [*de bien jouer à la Dangeau*. Dangeau was a very skilful and successful gambler at the court of Louis XIV]. The game is quick; it may be said to stand halfway between piquet and games of chance."

In Paris, gambling of all kinds was freely indulged

in during the occupation by the Allied Armies, and after the peace. Many gambling houses in Paris were licensed and farmed from 1818 to 1837, and besides these licensed houses there were numerous "*maisons de bouillote et d* baccarat*," which, though unlicensed, were tolerated by and under the surveillance of the police. At these houses private play went on almost unchecked, and, according to Boiteau, Écarté was a very favourite game there (*on y jouait surtout à l'Écarté*). But before the game changed its name and got into the *Salons*, it is probable that, like Whist, it ran through various grades of society, being first played by the peasantry (Berni). It then became a *jeu d'antichambre;* Bescherelle, *Dictionnaire National* (fifth edition, 1857), says, "*Écarté.—L'origine de ce jeu n'est rien moins que noble; il ne fût pas d'abord en usage que chez les laquais;*" after that it was a *jeu de fripon*, and was still so regarded for a considerable time.

Gabriel Peignot (*Analyse de toutes les Recherches sur les Cartes à jouer*, 1826), quotes a periodical relative to the social changes that took place in France after the Revolution, which says, "Écarté has appeared, * * * everybody flocks round the Écarté tables." And Lieut.-Col. Read, in *Rouge et Noir* (third edition, London, 1830), which describes the doings at Frascati's, the Palais Royal gaming tables, and the Salons, says, "Some years ago *Rouge et Noir* was frequently introduced at the *soirée*, and dealers from the public tables employed to officiate. The practice is now interdicted, and *Écarté* prevails.

* * * It is quite a *tour de passe-passe* now." Everyone knows how the young Duke, in Disraeli's novel (published in 1831), was swindled at Écarté.

The evidence, so far as it goes, leads to the conclusion that Écarté was invented, or, at all events, first played by the higher classes in the Paris Salons in the first quarter of the nineteenth century. Thence it was, no doubt, brought to England. The author was informed by the late Mr. Bushe that when he made the *grand tour* of Europe, he first saw Écarté played in Paris. This must have been shortly after Waterloo. He thought it so good a game, that he intended on his return to England to propose its introduction at the clubs, but on entering White's he found he had been forestalled, that the same idea had occurred to another traveller who got home before him, and that everybody at White's was playing the new game. This fixes pretty accurately the time when Écarté crossed the Channel. It is hardly necessary to add that the game soon became popular; that it is much played at present is proved by the fact that the principal London Clubs have now (1877) deemed it advisable to promulgate a Code of Laws.

DESCRIPTION OF THE GAME.

INTRODUCTORY.

The Game of Écarté is played by two persons (but see p. 35). A pack of cards is required from which the sixes, fives, fours, threes, and twos have been thrown out. It is more convenient to have two packs, each being used alternately. The packs should be differently marked or coloured on the backs.

DEALING.

The players having cut for deal, the pack is shuffled, and the non-dealer cuts it. The dealer re-unites the packets, and gives five cards to each player. The cards are not dealt singly, but by two at a time to each, and then by three at a time to each, or *vice versâ*. In whichever manner the dealer commences to distribute the cards he must continue, *i.e.*, he must not deal at one time two and three, and at another three and two.

The eleventh card, now the top of the pack, is turned up for trumps. Should it happen to be a king, the dealer marks one; otherwise the turn-up is of no value; it merely indicates the trump suit for that deal. The remainder of the pack after the trump card is turned up is called the *stock*. The stock should be placed to the dealer's left. (*See* also Laws 1–22, pp. 7–10.)

DISCARDING.

The players now look at their hands. Should the non-dealer be satisfied with his cards, he may at once proceed to play them. But if he considers it to his advantage to exchange any or all of them, he *proposes*, saying, "I propose," or "Cards."

If the non-dealer proposes, the dealer has the option of *accepting* or *refusing*. If he accepts he may change any or all of his cards, and he signifies his intention of doing so by saying, "I accept," or "How many?" But if the dealer is satisfied with his hand he refuses to give cards, saying, "I refuse," or "Play."

If the non-dealer plays without proposing, the dealer must also play without exchanging any cards.

When a proposal is accepted, the non-dealer separates from his hand the number of cards he desires to exchange, and places them face downwards on the table to his right, at the same time naming the number discarded. The dealer also puts out his discard, and places it to his right, keeping it separate from his adversary's discard. The trump card is put aside, and the cards required by the non-dealer to restore the number in hand to five again are given him from the top of the stock. The dealer then helps himself to the number he has discarded.

If the non-dealer is still dissatisfied, he may propose a second time, saying, "Again," and the dealer may accept or refuse as before; and so on until the non-dealer has a hand that he wishes to play, or until the dealer refuses. (*See* also Laws 26–38, pp. 11–13.)

MARKING THE KING.

After the discard, or, if there is no discard, after the deal, the non-dealer, if he holds the king of trumps in his hand, should announce it, saying, " I have the king," or "King," and mark one. He must announce the king before playing a card, unless the card first played is the king, when he may announce it at any time before the dealer plays to it.

If the dealer has the king of trumps in his hand, he similarly announces it, and marks one. If it is the card he first plays, he may announce it at any time before he plays a second card. (*See* also Laws 22–25, p. 10.)

PLAYING.

The players having discarded or not, as they think proper, the non-dealer leads any card he chooses. His adversary plays a card to it; the two cards thus played constitute a *trick*.

The second player must not *renounce* if he holds a card of the suit led—*i.e.*, he is bound to follow suit, if able; and he must win the trick if he can. The highest card of the suit led wins the trick. The cards rank in the following order, beginning with the highest, king, queen, knave, ace, ten, nine, eight, seven. Trumps win other suits. Failing the suit led, the second player, if he has a trump, must win the trick by trumping. The winner of the trick leads to the next, and so on till the hand is played out. (*See* also Laws 39–43, pp. 13, 14.)

SCORING.

The score accrues from turning up or holding the king, as before explained, and from winning the majority of tricks.

The player who wins three tricks out of the five gains the *point*, and scores one. If he wins all five tricks he gains the *vole*, and scores two. Winning four tricks is no better than winning three.

If the non-dealer plays without proposing, and fails to make three tricks, his adversary scores two, just the same as though he had won a vole. Losing the vole is of no further consequence in this case, as whether the adversary makes three tricks or five he scores two.

Similarly, if the dealer refuses cards, and fails to win three tricks, his adversary scores two.

The rule as to playing without proposing and as to refusing, only applies to the first proposal or refusal in each hand. Playing without proposing a second time, or refusing a second proposal, does not entail any penalty.

The game is five up : *i.e.*, the player who first obtains five wins the game.

By agreement singles, doubles, and trebles may be played, and rubbers also, as at Whist, if preferred, the player winning two games out of three winning the rubber. Rubbers are often played best of five, seven, or eleven games, with or without reckoning singles, doubles and trebles.

When a series of games is played, the deal may be alternate, no fresh cut for deal being made at the end of a game, or there may be a fresh cut for deal after every game, as agreed. If rubbers are played, the players cut for deal at the end of each game or rubber, as agreed. Sometimes the winner of the cut has choice of cards; this depends on previous agreement.

The score is most conveniently marked by means of counters, four being required by each player. The score should be marked to the player's right; and the counters not in use should be placed to his left. (And see Laws 46–51, pp. 14, 15.)

POOL ÉCARTÉ.

Sometimes Écarté is played by three persons. Each contributes a sum agreed on to form a *pool*. The players then cut ; the lowest is out, and the other two play one game, the highest dealing the first hand. The loser retires, and adds to the pool a sum equal to his first stake. The player who was out during the first game takes the loser's seat and cards, but cuts for deal, and plays with the winner of the first game. If the player who won the first game also wins the second, the loser adds another stake, the winner takes the pool, and a fresh one is commenced. But, if the winner of the first game loses the second, he adds a stake and retires, and the loser of the first game takes his place; and so on, until one player wins two games consecutively.

The mode of forming the pool is sometimes varied by only requiring the players engaged to contribute to the pool, the player who is out adding a stake each time he comes in. In this case, the loser does not add to the pool on his retirement.

The player who goes out after the first game may correct errors in the score; but he must not give advice on the conduct of the hand, unless the players have declared to play French Écarté.

FRENCH ÉCARTÉ.

At French Écarté there are generally one or more bystanders, who bet on the game, and some or all of these may be *rentrants, i.e.,* ready to take the place of the player they back, as soon as he goes out, or loses a game.

All the stakes and the betted money are placed on the table, and covered by the opposite side. The players have the right of taking all bets in preference to bystanders. If they do not take all, any bystander may take the difference, or the bystanders may make it up between them. If the whole of the betted money is not covered, the bettors of the larger amount take up so much of the sum they have put down as makes the amount on both sides equal.

At the end of the game, the winning player first takes up the amount he is entitled to, and the bettors then divide their share. If there is any deficiency in the amount, the player receives in full, and the bettors share the loss, *pro ratâ*, between them.

The losing player retires, and one of the *rentrants* takes his place. The *rentrants* must agree among themselves which shall go in; an order of going in being once established is adhered to, fresh *rentrants,* who have not played, having the preference over those who have.

Bystanders at French Écarté, who are covering the stakes, may draw attention to errors in the score, may advise the player they are backing (he being at liberty to follow the advice or not), or may play out the game of a player who resigns.   Advice must be given by pointing only; neither cards nor suit may be named.

If a player chooses to cover all the bets that are offered, called playing *La Chouette*, no one is at liberty to look over his hand, nor to advise him; and he does not retire after losing a game.

HINTS,

SHUFFLING.

1. The pack should be thoroughly shuffled after every deal. Otherwise, the cards are apt to get packed in suits in the course of play, and the trump card will not improbably be of the same suit as those preceding it, which are in the dealer's hand.

It is an act of courtesy to your adversary to shuffle your own pack well after every deal, that he may not have the trouble of making your cards for you.

LOOKING AT HAND.

2. The inexperienced player should be cautious not to let either his countenance or manner betray him. To this end, it is advisable for the dealer not to look at his hand until after his adversary has decided whether to propose or not.

ANNOUNCING.

3. A player holding the king should not announce it until he is in the act of playing his first card.

PROPOSING.

4. It is important to propose *quickly*, as hesitation exposes the nature of the hand. In order to be quick in proposing, the *Jeux de Règle* should be known by heart.

5. It is especially necessary to be prompt in proposing, when holding cards which make the point certain (*see* Hint 9 *a*, p. 41).

6. Some players have a trick of affecting to consider before proposing, though they hold but poor cards. It is only necessary to mention this manœuvre to condemn it, and to caution beginners against it.

DISCARDING.

7. The discard of less than three cards is almost always bad, unless you hold the king of trumps. With this card in hand you may discard freely, until you get cards that answer your purpose. For example : two small trumps and a guarded queen is a hand that should be played without proposing. But if one of the trumps is the king, cards should be asked for, unless the second card in the queen suit is at least as high as the ten, or the outside card is an honour. Hands which contain two trumps, with weak cards in plain suits (see *Jeux de Règle*, pp. 48–55), should be proposed on, whether one of the trumps is the king or not.

8. When discarding, throw out all cards except trumps and kings. Consequently, hands from which

only two cards can be discarded, without throwing a trump or a king, should be played without proposing. For it is almost certain that the adversary, if he accepts, will exchange more than two cards, and he may exchange four or five; hence, he has a better chance than the proposer of strengthening his hand, and of taking the king (but *see* Hint 9, *a*, *b*, *c*).

9. All hands should be played without proposing, when (the king of trumps not being in hand) the odds are two to one in favour of winning the point with the hand dealt. Some hands, from which only two cards can be discarded, are played, with which the odds are less than two to one in favour of winning the point. The reason for playing these is that, if you exchange, the chance of scoring will be more against you than it was before, even allowing for the penalty, if you fail to win the point.

All the hands that should be played without proposing, called *Jeux de Règle*, have been calculated. The *Jeux de Règle*, and the mode of playing them, are given at pp. 48–55. The only doubtful hand is three trumps and two sevens (*Jeu de Règle*, No. I., p. 48). This hand, against the best play, is about three to two in favour of the leader. Some players exchange two cards with this hand, but play it if either of the outside cards is higher than an eight.

Hands stronger than those given should, *a fortiori*, be played without proposing, with the following exceptions :—

a. If you hold the king of trumps and cards which ensure the point, you should propose, even for one card, unless you hold all court cards and trumps. For, by proposing, you have the chance of a refusal, which gives you two points on winning three tricks and, if the proposal is accepted and you take in one good card, it may give you the vole.

b. If you hold the king of trumps, and can only throw two cards without discarding a card at least as high as a ten from your guarded suit (*see* Hint 7, p. 39). For, though the odds are more than two to one in favour of your winning the point, your chance of scoring is increased by exchanging, taking into account the absence of penalty if you fail to win the point. There is also the chance of a refusal.

c. If you have proposed once, and, after discarding, you hold the king of trumps, and have the point certain, but with one or two weak unguarded cards, it is advisable to ask for cards a second time, for the chance of the vole.

10. A second proposal ought not to be made if the hand gives an even chance of winning the point (except as advised in Hint 9, *c*). The adversary having exchanged some cards, an even chance hand must contain cards somewhat stronger than those given as examples in Hint 21.

11. Before quitting the cards you discard, note the
suits to which they belong. This may be of use in
various ways. For example: you discard two hearts
and a diamond, and, having a heart and a diamond of
equal value in hand, are put to a card. Failing other
indications, you should keep the diamond. There
being more diamonds to account for than hearts, the
chances are in favour of your adversary's holding a
small diamond as against a small heart (*see* also Illustrative Hand, No. I., p. 58).

REFUSING.

12. The general rule is for the dealer to accept,
unless he is guarded in three suits, or is guarded in
two suits and has a trump, or is guarded in one suit
and has two trumps. He may play such hands with
rather weaker cards than the non-dealer.

13. It must be borne in mind that the dealer may
be forced before he gets the lead. Hence, if he is
only guarded in one suit with one trump, or in two
suits without a trump, he requires a stronger hand to
play than the non-dealer.

14. The rule not to discard two cards, unless holding the king of trumps, applies to the dealer (*see* also
Hands with which to Refuse, pp. 55–57).

PLAYING.

15. Holding three trumps it is almost always the
game to commence with a trump (but *see* Illustrative
Hand, No. III. With less than three trumps, you

should seldom lead a trump at starting, unless you hold king; or queen, knave; or knave, ace; with court cards out of trumps (see *Jeu de Règle*, No. III, and Illustrative Hand, No. I, for hands with which to commence with a trump).

16. With less than three trumps, the general system of play is to lead from two or more of a plain suit, and to lead the highest. The lead from the strong suit is the one most likely to force the adversary; and, if the trumps are equal, the first force will probably win the point.

17. There are, however, various exceptions to leading as directed in Hint 16. Thus :—You may hold such cards that, if the king is not declared against, you would lead a trump. If your high plain cards are of equal value, you should then lead the one which is least likely to be trumped, *i.e.*, the shortest suit (*see* Illustrative Hand, No. I). Again :—You may desire to keep a tenace, to be led to later in the hand. These positions often occur (*see* Illustrative Hands, Nos. IV, V, VI, VII). And again :—If cards are refused, you should generally lead from low cards in sequence rather than from a tenace. For instance :—You hold knave, nine of hearts; king of clubs; and eight, seven of diamonds. Spades are trumps. You propose and are refused. You should lead a diamond. Or :—You have king of spades (trumps); eight, seven of clubs; and queen and another heart. Cards are refused. You should lead the king of trumps, and then a club.

Another exception to leading the strong suit is, when playing a weak hand after a refusal, with no hope of the point and fear of the vole. You should then lead your highest single card, so that your guarded suit may be led to. For example:—You have a queen single; a queen guarded; and two worthless cards. Cards are refused. You should lead the single queen.

The above does not apply to a guarded king, which in such case should be led at once. Having only one queen guarded, or one knave guarded, with a weak hand, and cards being refused, it is never right to lead the guarded card.

18. If the strong suit is led, and is not trumped, it should, as a rule, be persevered with.

19. There are many exceptions to Hint 18. Thus:— If the leader has the king of trumps; or queen (king not having been announced in the other hand); or knave, ace; it would often be right to lead trumps before going on with the suit (see, however, Illustrative Hands, Nos. I, II).

Again:—When playing for the vole, with a weak trump and high cards in other suits, you should change the suit each time as the best chance of avoiding a ruff. If three tricks are made in this way, then the single trump should be led.

And again:—You play on two trumps with a tenace; two cards of another suit, and one outside card as high as a nine or ten. The first trick is won by you in your guarded suit, and the king is declared adversely. You should now lead your single card (see Illustrative Hands, Nos. VIII and IX).

Changing the suit is often advisable, in order to

avoid being put to a card at the end of the hand (*see* Illustrative Hands, Nos. X, XI).

20. During the play of the hand, the number of tricks made by each player will often direct as to the next lead. For instance :—Each player has made one trick. The leader has a high tenace in trumps, and one other card. It is obvious that he should lead the outside card.

Or :—The adversary has declared the king. The leader has won two tricks, and remains with queen and two small trumps. By leading a small trump he must make the point.

Again :—You have won two tricks, your opponent one, and you hold a trump and a plain card. Your lead is the plain card. But if your adversary has won two tricks, and you win the third, and remain with a trump and a plain card, your lead is the trump (though only the seven), in hopes of putting him to a card.

And again :—Having made two tricks, and finding the adversary has no trump, it is better to lead a king than a trump. Then lead the trump, and the adversary, if he has another card of your king suit, will be in doubt whether to keep that suit or not; whereas, had the trump been led first, he would unhesitatingly have kept the suit in which he was guarded. The principal advantage of this mode of play is when the king led is guarded. But the king should equally be played if single, as, if the method is only pursued when the king is guarded, the adversary will, of course, keep that suit.

EFFECT OF THE SCORE.

21. When the dealer is at four, and the king is not in your hand nor turned up, you should play any cards without proposing which give an even chance of three tricks, *e.g.*, a queen, a guarded knave, and a guarded ten without a trump; or, one trump, ace of one plain suit, and a guarded ten of another. In the language of the card-table, "play a light hand against four." If the point is lost, the adversary wins the game in any case (the penalty of his scoring two for the point is inoperative), and by not changing cards all chance of his taking the king is avoided. When the non-dealer is at four, the dealer should also refuse on a light hand; but he ought to have some protection in three suits, as, for instance, three knaves, or a knave and two guarded tens.

22. The dealer being at four, and the king not being in your hand nor turned up, you should play any hand which contains one trump, unless the cards out of trumps are of different suits and very small (*see* Hint 21); similarly, the dealer should refuse cards, if he holds a trump when his adversary is at four. With one trump and four small cards of a suit, the non-dealer should play at this point of the game, but the dealer should not.

23. If the dealer is at four, the rule to ask for cards with three certain tricks in hand (*see* Hint 9*a*, p. 41) does not hold, unless the player proposing has the king of trumps, or king is turned up.

24. If the non-dealer plays without proposing when he is at four to the dealer's three, the dealer, if he holds the king, ought not to mark it; for if he wins the point he scores two and the game; and marking the king would unnecessarily expose his hand. The same rule applies to the non-dealer, if the dealer refuses cards when he is at four and his opponent at three.

25. At the same score (dealer four to three), the dealer should refuse on a light or even chance hand (*see* Hint 21) notwithstanding that the loss of the point will then lose him the game. The reason is that the player proposing at this score must have very bad cards. This rule, though important, is often disregarded, even by players of some experience.

26. At four, a forward game should not be played in trumps, as there is no advantage in winning the vole. Thus with *Jeu de Règle* No. 6, p. 51, if the trump is the queen, the leader at this score should continue the suit, and not play the trump after passing the king of his suit. By playing in this way it is possible to make three tricks, even against two trumps in the other hand. For, if the adversary holds knave and another trump, and trumps the second card of the strong suit, he may lead his knave to pass his other cards. If he does so he loses the point (*see* also Illustrative Hands, Nos. I, II, and XIV.)

JEUX DE REGLE.

HANDS TO BE PLAYED WITHOUT PROPOSING.

[Spades are trumps throughout. The score is assumed to be Love-all.]

No. 1.

Any hand with three or more trumps.

Some players exchange two cards with this hand, if the outside cards are of different suits and neither is as high as a nine.

Lead the highest trump,

If one of the trumps is the king, or if king is turned up, ask for cards, as then there is no risk of the opponent's taking the king.

No. 2.

Two trumps, and three cards of a suit.

Lead the highest card of the suit not trumps, and continue until trumped.

If one of the trumps is the king, ask for cards.

No. 3.

Two trumps, queen and another of a suit, and a small card of a third suit.

This is a *Jeu de Règle*, but some players are afraid to risk it without another card as high as a ten, in lieu of one of the small cards.

If the trumps are high, the guarded queen should be led. If the trumps are low, commence with the single card, in hopes of forcing the adversary, and of being led to in the guarded suit. This is an exception to the rule of commencing with the guarded suit.

If one of the trumps is the king, ask for cards. But with king and another trump, queen and another card of the same suit at least as high as the ten, or queen and a small card in one suit with an honour in the other suit, the hand should be played.

With queen in each of the three suits, begin with the queen of trumps, as, if the king is encountered, the other suits are led up to.

If the guarded plain card is a king, lead the king.

D

No. 4.

Two trumps, eight, seven of a suit, and king of a third suit.

If the guarded cards are in sequence, lead that suit; but if not, lead the single king.

If one of the trumps is the king, ask for cards.

With similar but rather stronger hands—as, for example, king and another trump, queen, knave of the second suit, and a knave—commence with the guarded queen, and then, if it wins, lead the king of trumps. To start with the king of trumps for the vole is too risky.

Hands of intermediate strength between No. 3 and No. 4 should be played, viz : two trumps, knave, ace of one suit, and nine or eight of another; or ace, ten of one suit, and ace or ten of another; or ten, nine of one suit and knave of another; or nine, eight of one suit, and queen of another.

Some players will not risk two trumps, knave, ace of one plain suit and an outside eight; or ace, ten of one suit and an outside ten.

With all the above hands, begin with the guarded plain suit.

No. 5.

Two trumps, a king, a knave, and an eight or seven of different suits.

Lead the single king.

Similarly, hands containing king, ace, nine, of different suits, or king and two tens of different suits from the king, should be played.

Also hands containing two queens; queen, knave, ace of different suits; or three court cards, should be played.

With such hands the highest single card should be led (but *see* Illustrative Hand, No. VI).

No. 6.

One trump, a tierce major, and a small card of a third suit.

Lead one of the tierce, and continue the suit. If trumped, the lead is regained with the trump. If not trumped, play the tierce major and then the trump.

If the trump is the king, commence with the trump.

If the trump is the queen, and the king is not declared after the first lead, the queen should be led, except at the point of four (*see* Effect of the Score, pp. 46, 47).

With king, queen, and a small card of the strong suit, the hand should not be played unless the other card out of trumps is an honour, or the cards held are king, queen, ace, and eight or nine of the third suit; or king, queen, ten, and another ten.

No. 7.

One trump, and king with three small cards of the same suit as the king.

Lead the king, and continue the suit.

If the trump is the king, ask for cards.

If the trump is the queen and the king is not declared after the first lead, the queen should be led, except at the point of four (*see* Effect of the Score, pp. 46, 47).

No. 8.

One trump, a queen single, and a queen with two small cards.

Start with the guarded queen, and continue the suit. If the suit is trumped, play it again on obtaining the lead.

If the trump is the king, ask for cards, unless the guard to the queen is at least as high as the ten.

If each queen is singly guarded, ask for cards, unless one of the guards is at least as high as the ten.

No. 9.

Four court cards, except the four knaves; but play four knaves if the knave of trumps is guarded (*Jeu de Règle* No. 5).

As a general rule, these hands should be played by commencing with the guarded card of the strongest suit out of trumps.

No. 10.

Hands from which only two cards can be discarded without throwing a king or a trump; also hands guarded by a queen in three suits, *i.e.*, with three queens.

The same general rule as before. Thus, with no trump and three queens, begin with a guarded queen.

No one can make an Écarté player without knowing the *Jeux de Règle*, and being able to recognise them at a glance. As an aid to the memory, the *Jeux de Règle* may be classified thus :—

1. All hands with *three trumps*.
2. Hands with *two trumps*, which contain also—
   a. Three cards of one suit.
   b. Two cards of one suit, one being as high as a queen.
   c. Two small cards of one suit, the fifth card being a king.
   d. Hands intermediate between *b* and *c* (see *Jeu de Règle* No. 4, p. 50).
   e. Three cards of different suits, as high as king, knave, and a small card, or of equivalent trick-making value (see *Jeu de Règle* No. 5, p. 51).
3. Hands with *one trump*, which contain also—
   a. A tierce major.
   b. Four cards of one suit, one being a king.
   c. Three cards of one suit, one being as high as a queen, and the fifth card being a queen.
4. Hands with *no trump*, which contain four court cards, or three queens.

It will be observed that (except when the king is taken into consideration,) the value of the trumps does not influence any of the hands which should be played without proposing. The reason is that it is

scarcely ever the game to lead trumps originally with
two trumps, neither being the king. The general
scheme of the game is to get the first force on the
dealer, and to use the trumps for trumping his winning cards. For this purpose high trumps are no
better than low ones.

The classification of the *Jeux de Règle* is therefore
based on the *number* of trumps held and not on their
value. The non-dealer should be guided in deciding
whether to propose by the number of trumps he holds,
and by the value of the plain cards, and by whether
they belong to one or more suits.

HANDS WITH WHICH TO REFUSE.

When a proposal is made it may be assumed that
the non-dealer has not a *Jeu de Règle*. The chance of
his having a very strong hand with the point certain
may be disregarded, as the cases are few in which,
with a refusal, he will only make three or four tricks
and not the vole, though had the proposal been accepted the vole would have been saved.

Or, the non-dealer may propose when he ought not,
through imperfect knowledge of the game. This consideration may also be dismissed, as in the long run
he will play at a disadvantage if he proposes when he
should not.

Taking into account that the non-dealer who proposes cannot hold any of the *Jeux de Règle*, it so
happens that the hands which give the dealer a two-
to-one chance of winning the point are not unlike
those on which the non-dealer should play (but *see*

Hints 12, 13, p. 42). It will be sufficient then, in order to arrive at the refusal hands, to comment on the *Jeux de Règle*, seriatim.

No. 1.—Three trumps, and any two plain cards.

Refuse, unless one of the trumps is the king.

No. 2.—Two trumps, and three cards of one plain suit.

> This hand is not strong enough to refuse upon unless the plain suit is headed by a court card.

Accept if one of the trumps is the king.

Nos. 3 and 4.—Two trumps, queen guarded of one suit, and a small card of another.

Two trumps, two small cards of one suit, and the king of another.

> These should be played, as also the intermediate hands given after *Jeu de Règle* No. 4 (p. 50).
> In all the above, if the king of trumps is in hand, accept.

No. 5.—Two trumps, and one card of each of the other suits as high as those given under *Jeu de Règle* No. 5 (p. 51) should be played.

No. 6.—One trump, a tierce major in one suit, and a small card of another.

> This should not be played unless the single card is a court card. With similar hands, but weaker in the tierce major suit, as given under *Jeu de Règle* No. 6 (pp. 51-52), accept, unless the single card is as high as a queen.

No. 7.—One trump with four cards of a plain suit headed by a king, is too weak to be played.

No. 8.—One trump, a single queen, and a queen with two guards.

> This hand should not be played. But refuse if both queens are singly guarded.
>
> Also, with one trump, queen of one suit, and knave and a small card of another, play the hand if the fifth card is of the same suit as the queen, or if it is a court card.
>
> In both the above hands, if the trump is the king give cards.
>
> One trump and two kings should be played, whatever the other cards; but one trump, a king and a queen of different suits, both unguarded, though it looks a strong hand, ought not to be played unless the guarded card of the fourth suit is at least as high as an ace. If the king or queen instead of being single is guarded, the hand should be played whatever the value of the fifth card.

No. 9.—Four court cards and no trump.

> If the court cards are of three different suits refuse, but if not, give cards.

No. 10.—Refuse with three queens if two are singly guarded, otherwise accept. Also, refuse on all hands from which only two cards can be discarded without throwing a king or a trump, unless the king of trumps is in hand.

ILLUSTRATIVE HANDS.

HAND I.

NON-DEALER'S HAND.

A small spade turned up.

This is a *Jeu de Règle.*

The game is to play without proposing, and to lead the knave of spades for the chance of the vole.

But if the hand is held after taking cards, the leader's object should be to ascertain whether his adversary has the king of trumps, as if not he should play for the vole.

The leader should, therefore, commence with the king that is least likely to be trumped. If he has not discarded a heart he should therefore lead the king of hearts. If the heart is not trumped and the king of trumps is not declared, the next lead should be the trump for the vole.

But if the king of hearts is trumped, all chance of the vole is lost, and the object then is to secure the point.

Suppose now the adversary leads a diamond. This must be trumped with the ten of spades.

The proper lead now is the king of clubs, and, if it passes, the ten.

The knave of trumps should not be led after the force, for if the adversary lies with queen of trumps and cards of the diamond suit, the leader loses the point.

It does not follow that the dealer would lead the queen of trumps if he had it. Indeed, if he is a good player he would not, as by holding it up he may induce the non-dealer to believe he has not got it, and to lead the knave (*see* Hint 26, p. 47).

HAND II.

NON-DEALER'S HAND.

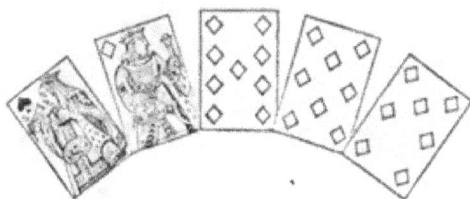

A small spade turned up.

This is a *Jeu de Règle*.

If the adversary is at four, it is a common error to begin with the queen of trumps.

Three tricks may be lost by leading the queen of trumps, if the adversary has no trump and two diamonds. Three tricks cannot be lost against this hand if the leader commences, as he should do, with the king and another diamond.

Moreover, three tricks *may* be won against two trumps by not leading the queen, and this *cannot possibly* be done by leading it. Thus, suppose the adversary has no diamond and knave and another trump. He trumps the king of diamonds, and, unless a good player, may lead knave of trumps to pass his other cards. Many a game has been lost in this manner, in consequence of the dealer's assuming that the queen is not in the non-dealer's hand, because it was not led originally (compare Example I, and Hint 26, p. 47).

HAND III.

Non-Dealer's Hand.

A small club turned up.

The non-dealer's score is three; he marks the king, making him four, and of course plays without proposing.

He should now make *certain* of the point. This

he can only do by leading the seven of spades. If he leads any other card it is possible that he may lose the point.

Thus :—The dealer has four trumps and a spade. He wins the first trick in spades, and, whatever he leads, the non-dealer must make three tricks.

If the non-dealer begins with a trump, and finds four trumps and a spade against him, he loses the point. The same if he begins with the king of diamonds, and the dealer, after trumping it, leads his spade.

There are many similar hands. For example, at the same score, holding king, knave, ten of trumps, a king of one plain suit, and a small card of a third suit, the only lead which makes a certainty of the point is the small card of the third suit.

Say the third suit is diamonds, and that the dealer has queen and two other trumps, and two diamonds, one of which is higher than the non-dealer's. If any card but the small diamond is led, the dealer wins the point.

The lead should be the same with king, queen and a small trump, or with king, knave and a small trump.

The object aimed at by the non-dealer is to be led to on the second trick. If he wins the second trick with his plain-suit king, and has a tenace in trumps, he leads the under trump; if he is forced on the second trick, and has a tenace in trumps, he then leads his outside card.

With such hands, and any two outside cards of different suits, and only wanting the point, the best chance is to lead the *lower* of the two plain cards, notwithstanding the general rules to lead a trump holding three trumps, and to begin with the highest card in hand when a trump is not led. If one of the plain cards is a king, there is no combination by which the leader can lose in consequence of first leading the other plain card. If the higher outside plain card is not a king, the point may sometimes be lost in consequence of first leading the lower card. It is, however, more advantageous to run this risk than to lead the higher of the two plain cards.

HAND IV.

NON-DEALER'S HAND.

A club turned up.

This is a *Jeu de Règle.*

The leader having a tenace in spades should lead the single king. If the king wins, the spade suit must be opened. If the king is trumped and the adversary holds more than one spade, he will lead to the guarded suit.

If the spades were of equal value, the game would be to begin with the guarded suit.

HAND V.

NON-DEALER'S HAND.

A diamond turned up.

The non-dealer proposes (*see* Hint 9, *b*), and is refused. He should lead king of trumps and then the spades, his best chance being that the refusal was on one trump with strong hearts and clubs.

But if to the king of trumps the adversary throws a spade, it is almost certain that he is guarded in spades. Therefore, spade being played to the trump by the dealer, the second lead should be one of the outside cards.

HAND VI.

NON-DEALER'S HAND.

A diamond turned up.

This is a *Jeu de Règle.*

If the trumps are very high, lead a trump for the

vole. But, with a low tenace in trumps, the leader's object should be to keep the cards with which he is most likely to get the lead on the second trick, and to lose it on the third, so that his tenace may be led to.

Hence, with the above hand, the first lead should be knave of hearts. If it wins, the next lead should be king of spades. If the knave of hearts is taken and a spade is next led, the non-dealer should then lead nine of clubs.

HAND VII.

DEALER'S HAND.

A spade turned up.

The non-dealer leads the king of diamonds. The dealer trumps with the seven of spades.

The dealer should now lead a heart, keeping the tenace in clubs.

The same would apply if the dealer had a third club (not the queen), and only one heart (not the king).

HAND VIII.

A small card turned up.

This is a *Jeu de Règle.*

The non-dealer leads the king of spades. The dealer marks king of trumps and follows suit with the ten of spades.

The non-dealer should now lead the ten of diamonds. The object is to take the best chance of not forcing the dealer on the second trick, and not to have the lead after the third trick, so as to avoid leading up to the king of trumps and a possible tenace. If the king of trumps is not guarded, the non-dealer's second lead is immaterial.

Also, by leading the diamond the non-dealer may win the point against three trumps and a losing diamond. This he cannot possibly do if he continues with the spade.

With similar hands, the non-dealer should only change his suit when he has a tenace in trumps. If his trumps are of equal value, he should play to force in his guarded suit.

E

HAND IX.

A heart turned up.

This is a *Jeu de Règle*.

The non-dealer leads knave of clubs. The dealer follows suit with a small club, and declares the king of trumps.

The non-dealer should next lead the nine of diamonds.

If the king of trumps is unguarded, the second lead is immaterial. If guarded, the leader's best chance is for the nine of diamonds to be good or for it to force a trump.

Hands could easily be constructed in which the non-dealer loses by changing his suit with the above cards. But on calculation of the chances it will be found that playing as advised wins the point more frequently than it loses.

HAND X.

NON-DEALER'S HAND.

Hearts trumps.

The non-dealer proposes and is refused. He then leads king, queen of clubs, to both of which the dealer follows suit.

To win the point, the refusal must have been on two trumps, two clubs and a losing spade or diamond.

If a third club is now led and the dealer is forced, he leads a trump, and the non-dealer is put to a card. To avoid this dilemma the non-dealer should now change his suit, and instead of leading the nine of clubs should lead one of his outside cards.

HAND XI.

DEALER'S HAND.

Diamonds trumps.

The non-dealer plays without proposing, and leads

a medium trump.   The dealer wins it, and opens his
guarded suit, and wins the second trick.

The probability is the non-dealer played on three
trumps.   To win the point his outside card must be
either a losing heart or a losing club.   Therefore the
dealer's next lead should be one of his tens.   If the
dealer forces with the spade, and a trump is then led,
he will be put to a card.

HAND XII.

DEALER'S HAND.

A small heart turned up.

If the non-dealer leads seven of spades, the dealer,
without hesitation, should win it with the king instead
of with the nine.

The game being to lead the highest of a suit, the
dealer may be certain that his adversary holds no card
between the one led and the king, except the eight,
which is of equal value.   The dealer, therefore, runs
no risk in winning the seven with the king.   It being
the rule to lead from a guarded suit, it is also pretty
certain that the non-dealer holds the eight, and has no
better plain suit of two cards.

By winning a low card with the highest in hand, instead of with a lower one, a point may sometimes be gained against a player who is unacquainted with the *ruse*, which would otherwise have been lost.

For example : suppose the non-dealer's hand to be eight, seven of spades, queen of hearts (trumps), queen of clubs, and queen of diamonds.

He leads the seven of spades. The dealer takes it with the king, and leads knave of clubs. This is won by the queen.

The non-dealer then leads queen of trumps and eight of spades, presuming as the seven forced the king that the eight is a winning card.

The dealer takes this with the nine of spades, and leads nine of clubs, which wins the third trick and the point.

Now, observe, had the dealer won the seven of spades with the nine, the non-dealer might have played differently, and have won the point. For, after winning a second trick with the . queen of trumps, he would remain with the eight of spades and the queen of diamonds. There are five spades superior to the eight, any one of which the non-dealer may hold, and only one diamond superior to the queen. The best chance therefore of winning one more trick (and consequently the point) with these cards, at this juncture, would be to lead the queen of diamonds.

HAND XIII.

DEALER'S HAND.

A small heart turned up.

The non-dealer commences with the king of trumps. The dealer should throw the queen to it.

The dealer's object is to persuade the leader to continue trumps, so that the lead may come into the dealer's hand before he is forced. If he throws the seven to the king, it is not improbable that his adversary, fearing trumps and clubs, may proceed with forcing cards. But if the queen is thrown, and the non-dealer has three trumps, he is very likely to lead another trump, hoping to get discards which may give him the vole. This may lose him the point. Thus, suppose he has ace, ten of trumps remaining, and two good cards in the spade or diamond suits. If he goes on with the trump he only makes one more trick, even if he holds kings or queens in the spade or diamond suits. With such a hand as king, ace, ten of trumps, and two kings or queens, he would play unwisely to continue the trump after the fall of the queen, as he has nothing to gain by it and may lose; but with smaller cards his best chance of the vole would be to persevere with the trump.

HAND XIV.

NON-DEALER'S HAND.

A small spade turned up.

Score, four-all. The non-dealer proposes and is refused.

The general rule is not to play a forward game at the score of four. But here, if the adversary has no trump he must have refused because he is guarded in all three suits. Hence the only chance of the point is for the refusal to have been on one trump smaller than the nine, with good clubs and diamonds, and no heart.

The non-dealer should therefore lead the nine of trumps.

CURRENT ODDS AT ÉCARTÉ.

The deal is no advantage at Écarté, notwithstanding that the dealer's chance of marking the king, as against the non-dealer's, is 66 to 35, or not quite 2 to 1. This advantage, however, in the opinion of experienced players, is, if anything, rather more than counterbalanced by the advantages of the lead and of the option of proposing.

The odds—in the language of Écarté players—are always " on the table," *i.e.*, the score each player has to make may be laid against him. For instance, when the scores are equal, no odds can be laid at any score ; at one to love, it is 5 to 4 on the player who has scored ; at three against one, it is 4 to 2 ; and so on. The layer of odds is considered to have a slight advantage throughout, except at the point of three with the deal against two, when 3 to 2 is rather more than the proper odds ; also at four with the deal to three, it is disadvantageous to lay 2 to 1.

TABLE OF ODDS.

SCORE.	ODDS.	SCORE.	ODDS.
Love-all ...	Even	2 all	Even
1 to 0 ...	5 to 4	3 to 2 ...	*3 to 2
2 to 0 ...	5 to 3	4 to 2 ...	3 to 1
3 to 0 ...	5 to 2		
4 to 0 ...	5 to 1		
		3 all	Even
1 all	Even	4 to 3 ...	†2 to 1
2 to 1 ...	4 to 3		
3 to 1 ...	4 to 2		
4 to 1 ...	4 to 1	4 all	Even

* Bad to lay if 3 has the deal.   † Bad to lay if 4 has the deal.